i

Colorful Animals

Élisabeth de Lambilly-Bresson

GARETH**STEVENS**

PUBLISHING

A Member of the WRC Media Family of Companies

The Panther

I am a panther.
I am a big, wild cat
with long, sharp teeth.
My fur is thick and black.
When I move quickly
and quietly through the forest,
my glowing eyes see everything.

The Parakeets

We are blue parakeets.
You can teach us to talk.
We like to chatter a lot.
We even talk to mirrors!
We are easy to tame
and can be good company.
Hello!
Please give us some crackers.

The Clown Fish

I am a clown fish.
My orange and white stripes
are so colorful
you might think
I am dressed for the circus.
When I want to have fun,
I play hide-and-seek
in the sea.

The Chick

I am a chick.
I am yellow from my head
to my short, sticklike legs.
I follow behind my mother hen,
looking on the ground
for seeds to peck and eat.
Cheep! Cheep! Cheep!

The Seal

I am a baby seal.
My thick, white fur
helps me hide in the snow
and keeps me warm in the wind.
I like to be warm.
Where I live,
it feels like winter all the time!

The Flamingo

I am a pink flamingo.
My long legs look like stilts.
My neck bends
like a garden hose.
Shrimp is my favorite treat.
It makes me as pink as a rose,
from my crooked beak
to the tips of my toes.

The Lizard

I am a green lizard.
I like to sleep in the sunlight.
When I lie on a log or a rock,
the sunshine keeps me warm.
But if you wake me,
I will dash away
in a flash!

Please visit our Web site at: www.garethstevens.com
For a free color catalog describing Gareth Stevens Publishing's
list of high-quality books and multimedia programs, call
1-800-542-2595 (USA) or 1-800-387-3178 (Canada).
Gareth Stevens Publishing's fax: (414) 332-3567.

Library of Congress Cataloging-in-Publication Data

Lambilly-Bresson, Elisabeth de.
  [Tout en couleurs. English]
  Colorful animals / Elisabeth de Lambilly-Bresson. — North American ed.
    p. cm. — (Animal show and tell)
  ISBN-13: 978-0-8368-8159-2 (lib. bdg.)
  1. Animals—Color—Juvenile literature. I. Title.
QL767.L2713 2007
591—dc22
                            2006033118

This edition first published in 2007 by
Gareth Stevens Publishing
A Member of the WRC Media Family of Companies
330 West Olive Street, Suite 100
Milwaukee, WI 53212 USA

Translation: Gini Holland
Gareth Stevens editor: Gini Holland
Gareth Stevens art direction and design: Tammy West

This edition copyright © 2007 by Gareth Stevens, Inc. Original edition copyright
© 2002 by Mango Jeunesse Press. First published as *Les animinis: Tout en couleurs*
by Mango Jeunesse Press.

Printed in the United States of America

1 2 3 4 5 6 7 8 9 10 10 09 08 07 06